TopReaders

Getting in Touch

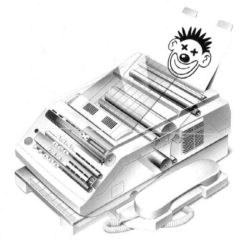

Kate McAllan

Contents

Like other animals, humans tell
each other things with their voices
and by the looks on their faces.
People have also worked out ways to
get in touch when they are too far
apart to talk with or to see each other.

Wolves

Wolves can make their voices carry a long way by howling. They howl to stay in touch with each other. A lone wolf howls to find other members of its pack. When wolves kill an animal, they howl to tell the rest of the pack where to join them to eat.

Wolves in a pack howl together to warn other wolves to stay out of their territory.

Spoken Word

Unlike other animals, humans use their voices to speak. They can tell each other exactly what they have thought about, seen, or done. People who did not use writing, such as American Indians, passed on messages by remembering what someone else had said.

☆ **Fact File**

Some American Indian stories tell of mammoth attacks. Mammoths died out 12,000 years ago.

American Indian storytellers tell their stories many times. This helps other people learn and remember them.

Hieroglyphs

In ancient Egypt , people used hieroglyphs, a kind of writing based on pictures. Hieroglyphs allowed them to record facts, ideas, and stories. Egyptians carried letters to distant places, and wrote about their gods on temple walls for others to read.

☆ **Fact File**

The first hieroglyphs date from about 5,300 years ago. They list items given to a king.

In ancient Egypt, scribes were the only people who could read and write. Boys took many years to learn how to become scribes.

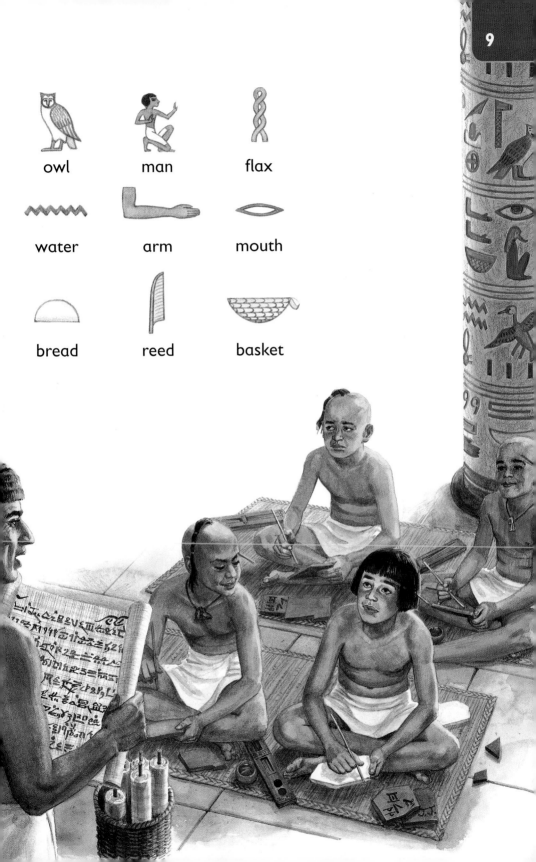

owl

man

flax

water

arm

mouth

bread

reed

basket

Written Word

Writing in China began more than 3,000 years ago. First the people carved writing into stone or strips of bamboo. Then they used ink to write on silk and paper. Written messages from the emperor were carried all over the Chinese empire to be read.

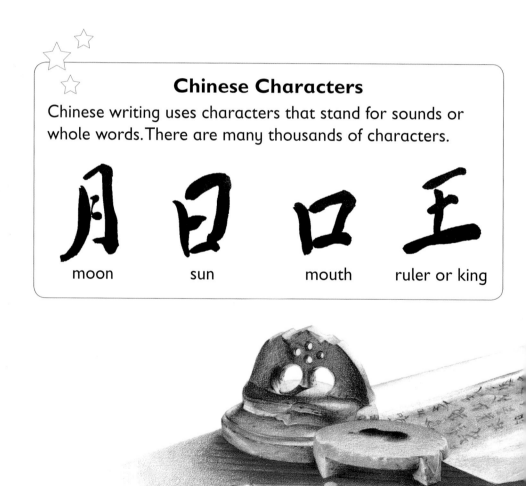

Chinese Characters

Chinese writing uses characters that stand for sounds or whole words. There are many thousands of characters.

月 日 口 王

moon   sun   mouth   ruler or king

The ancient Chinese wrote with brushes made of animal hair and bamboo.

Carrying Messages

Written messages were carried from one person to another. Messengers walked, rode on horseback, or traveled by ship. But messengers and their letters did not always safely reach where they were meant to go.

Africa

Australia

A bottle was thrown into the sea near South America.

South America

Letters put in bottles and thrown into the sea can travel a long way, but no one knows where they will go.

Hawaii

Three years later, the bottle reached Easter Island.

Early Telephones

In 1876, Alexander Graham Bell invented a machine called a telephone. It turned sounds into electrical signals that went along a wire, then turned back into sounds at the other end. Using telephones, people could talk over long distances.

String Phone

Your voice travels as vibrations along a string from one can to another. It turns back into sound when it reaches the other end.

mouthpiece

dial

earpiece

Operators had to connect
phone lines themselves so
that people could speak
on the telephone.

Today's Telephones

Today, operators do not need to connect telephone calls. The wires are connected in automatic telephone exchanges. A cell phone works by sending an electrical signal to a tower, which sends the signal to another phone. People can carry their cell phones wherever they go.

☆ Fact File

On April 3, 1973, Marty Cooper made the first call from a cell phone. His phone was heavy—it weighed 2 pounds (1 kg).

Cell phones do more than make phone calls. They can take and send pictures, and connect to the Internet.

Today's telephones have keypads to enter the telephone number.

Fax Machines

A fax machine uses a telephone line to send letters or pictures. This machine turns information on paper into electrical signals, and sends them along telephone lines. At the other end, the signals are turned into a printed copy, called a facsimile (or fax).

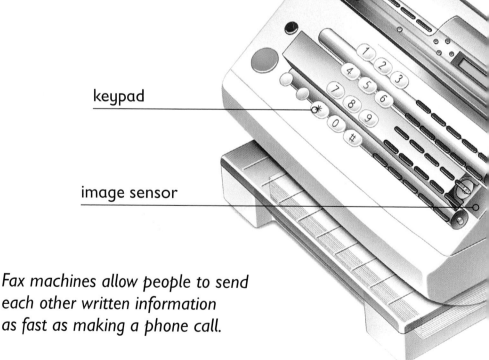

keypad

image sensor

Fax machines allow people to send each other written information as fast as making a phone call.

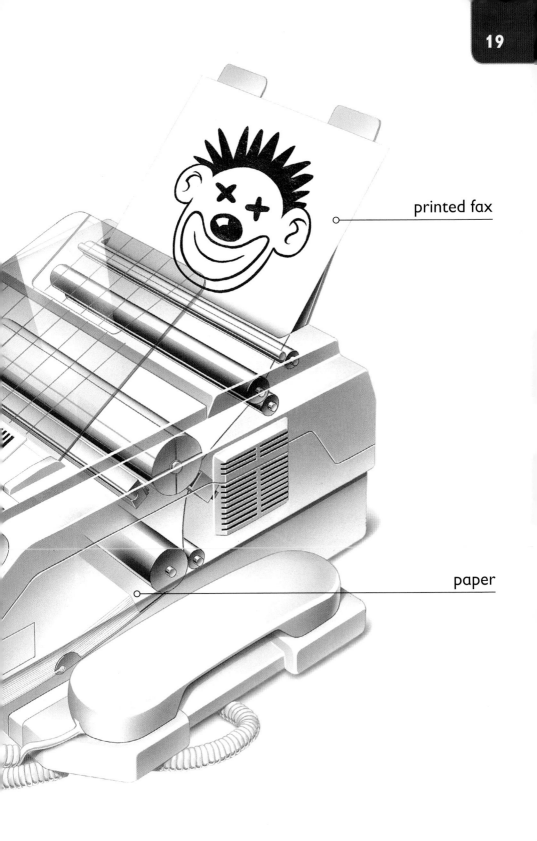

printed fax

paper

Radios

In the late 1800s, scientists worked out how to send sounds through the air with electrical signals called radio waves. In 1920 in the Netherlands, the first radio station began to send out, or broadcast, radio shows. During the 1920s, many people bought radios to listen to music programs, the news, and radio plays.

Lightweight Radios

In the 1960s, people made the first small, lightweight radios. They used batteries, and did not need to be plugged into electricity. They could be carried around outside.

In a modern radio studio, people talk into microphones and listen through headphones.

Televisions

Television stations use radio waves to send pictures as well as sound. Some television stations send signals through cables instead of through the air. Television allows people to see as well as hear what is happening on the other side of the world.

☆ Fact File

Television programs first appeared in the 1930s. Color televisions were first sold in the 1950s.

Plasma Screens

Plasma screens can be made much larger than ordinary television screens. They create bright colors and show fine details. Unfortunately, they use a lot of electricity, too.

Not many people had televisions until the 1950s.

flat-screen monitor ──────────────○

Computers

Using the Internet, computers can send vast amounts of information around the world in moments. They send sounds, writing, photographs, and even films. The Internet sends information as electronic signals. It uses telephone lines, cell phone equipment, or satellites .

tower

mouse

keyboard

The early computers of the 1940s were big—they filled whole
rooms. Today's computers are small enough to fit on a desk.

Messages from Space

Thousands of satellites orbit Earth. Radio and television signals are sent up to satellites, and they bounce back to other places in the world. Other satellites take pictures of the weather and send them to us.

Some satellites orbit Earth around the equator. Others go from pole to pole. Satellites travel about 5 miles (8 km) every second.

Radar

Radar works in a similar way to the sonar that bats
and dolphins use to find their food. A radio signal
is sent toward an object, such as a star or satellite.
When the radio signal hits the object, it bounces back.
The radar measures the time this takes. Then it can
work out where and how far away the object is.

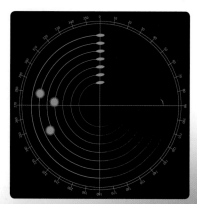

radar screen that
shows three objects

Radio telescopes send electronic signals into space. They also receive signals from satellites and natural objects , such as stars.

Quiz

Can you unscramble the words and match them with the right pictures?

TLESTILEA

ODIAR

HEPTELNEO

GHERPLHIOYS

Glossary

automatic: something that works without a person doing anything to make it happen

connect: to join together

Egypt: a country in the north of Africa. The Nile River flows through Egypt.

electrical: made by electricity

emperor: someone who rules a group of countries called an empire

fax: short for facsimile, which means copy

howl: to make a long, loud call that sounds like a wail

Internet: a system that joins computers around the world to each other

mammoth: a kind of elephant with long hair that lived long ago

natural objects: things that are not made by people

operators: people who work machines

orbit: to go around a planet or a star

satellites: spacecraft that go around Earth or another planet and that send information to Earth

scribes: people whose job it was to read and write for people who could not do so

signals: sounds, lights, or pictures that give a message

sonar: a way to navigate using sounds and echoes

Index